Temporal Enigma

Unraveling Mysteries Across Time

Contents Table

I. Introduction

A. Establish the Scene

1. Describe a strange incident that starts time travel.

2. Present the protagonist's realization of the talent.

II. The Mystery of Time

A. Dissecting the Guidelines

1. Specify the guidelines and restrictions for time travel.

2. The protagonist testing out his newly acquired abilities.

III. Discovery of Parallel Universes

A. Various Timelines

Examine alternate universes impacted by time travel.

2. The effects of changing the course of history.

IV. Historical Mysteries

A. Investigations using Time-Hopping

1. The protagonist does research in several eras of history.

2. Discover a centuries-spanning conspiracy.

V. Dangers of the Temporal Order

A. Agenda of the Opponent

1. Expose the evil scheme of the adversary, which involves temporal manipulation.

2. As their motivations become more apparent, up the ante.

Vi. Race Against Inconsistencies
A. Irregular Risks
1. Identify the risks involved in constructing temporal paradoxes.
2. Face the consequences as the past and the future converge.

VII. Betrayals and Allies
A. Temporal Partners
1. Introduce your allies from various eras.
2. Examine problems with trust and possible betrayals.

VIII. The Last Face-To-Face
A. Point of convergence
1. Convene all timelines for a dramatic confrontation.
2. The antagonist and protagonist engage in a conflict spanning time.

IX. Conclusion and Disclosure
1. End the temporal crisis by closing the time rift.
2. Discover the conclusive explanation for the conundrum of time travel.

X. Conclusion
A. Prospective Consequences
1. Take care of the fallout and residual consequences.
2. Make space for prospective follow-ups or spin-offs

Chapter 1: Introduction

A unexpected burst of energy interrupted the routine of a typical experiment in the calm halls of the scientific research facility, propelling our protagonist, Dr. Eleanor Reynolds, into the unknown realm of time. Shrouded in a mysterious light, the event not only defied physics but also created a portal to a realm where the past, present, and future came together to create a hypnotic dance.

Eleanor gains a surprising capacity to traverse the temporal threads that tie the cosmos as she struggles to make sense of this unexplainable event. Her surroundings change into a maze of options where every move reveals the complex dance between fate and time.

We travel through the Temporal Enigma in the upcoming chapters as Eleanor tries to decipher the laws guiding this newly acquired ability. She goes into unknown area, pushing the bounds of what is known and testing the very fabric of reality, from demonstrating the limitations of time travel to exploring the undiscovered depths of temporal manipulation.

We explore Parallel Universes Unveiled as the story progresses, where several timelines show the effects of changing the past. In Historical Intrigue, Eleanor delves into centuries-old mysteries through her time-traveling research, uncovering a plot entwined with the threads of history.

However, as an adversary's dark goal becomes apparent, Temporal Threats loom over this mysterious voyage. As motives become more apparent, the stakes rise and the tension grows, drawing Eleanor into a Race Against Paradoxes. In a thrilling crescendo, the risks of inventing temporal anomalies are revealed, as the consequences of tampering with the past and future collide.

The temporal volatility brings Betrayals and Allies to the fore. Eleanor's mission becomes more intricate as she meets companions from several timelines and navigates betrayals and trust difficulties.

The Final Confrontation, where all timelines collide for a dramatic conflict, is where the plot achieves its pinnacle. In a conflict that cuts across time, entwining the strands of the past, present, and future, Eleanor faces the enemy.

Eleanor is guided in Closing the Time Rift by Resolution and Revelation as the story comes to an end. The reader is left on the brink of discovery as the temporal crisis is resolved and the final piece of the time-traveling puzzle is revealed.

In the Conclusion, we finally discuss Eleanor's journey's Future Implications and examine the fallout and lasting consequences of her temporal adventure. The story ends by allowing opportunity for possible spin-offs or sequels, encouraging readers to consider the unknown possibilities that may yet arise.

Chapter 2: The Mystery of Time

The laws controlling this unknown power started to reveal themselves like old scrolls as Alex ventured farther into the fascinating field of time travel. It appeared that time was not simply twisted, and interfering with its delicate threads would have far-reaching and unpredictable effects.

Defining the guidelines and restrictions.

Scanning old manuscripts and scientific journals, Alex worked in the darkly lit study that smelled of books and was quiet enough to be filled with the gentle ticking of an antique clock. The text on the pages presented a patchwork of guidelines pertaining to time travel. It was not possible to jump through time without any repercussions. The future was a fragile web that was easily ripped apart, and the past was resistant to change.

Alex began to notice trends as she carefully typed out the guidelines. Avoiding paradoxes was imperative, as they had the capacity to shatter the foundation of existence. Moments in time that remained constant, akin to anchors in a raging ocean, established a cosmic order deserving of reverence. Alex realized the seriousness of this time obligation the more he studied the laws.

Protagonist Trying Out His Newfound Ability

Now that he was aware of these temporal laws, Alex found it difficult to avoid trying new things. The protagonist traveled into the unknown reaches of time during the calm moments of the night, when everyone else was asleep. Generation after generation, a pocket watch served as the channel for this newfound authority.

 The first leap was unsteady, a trip back in time to a moment that was meaningful to the individual. The world around Alex grew hazy as she felt the tickle of temporal energy, and then the past came to life like a vivid dream. But there were some difficulties with the experience. The laws made their presence felt, reshaping the route and placing restrictions that required cautious maneuvering.

Alex investigated the limits of his impact on historical events in subsequent experiments that stretched the boundaries even further. With every step into the time unknown, our comprehension of the complex dance between cause and effect grew. The main character struggled with the weight of decisions and the fallout that reverberated across time like echoes in a huge canyon.

Alex took comfort in knowledge-seeking as the temporal mystery developed, but one question remained unanswered: Was time a flexible fabric or a stiff framework that resisted the attempts of anyone who ventured to change its direction? The solutions remained evasive, concealed in the temporal enigma's shadows and waiting to be revealed in later chapters.

Chapter 3: Exposure of Parallel Universes

Alex fell into a rabbit hole of parallel universes and different realities as a result of the riddles surrounding time travel, which extended beyond the boundaries of a single timeline.

Examine Time-Transfer Affected Parallel Universes

Alex's comprehension of time grew, and the structure of reality started to break down. Once restricted to the domain of theoretical physics, parallel universes emerged into actuality. Every time jump caused a split in the cosmos, resulting in remnants of different histories that coexisted alongside our own.

 temporal nudges. The consequences of even the most minor alterations echoed across the multiverse, creating a kaleidoscope of worlds shaped by the choices made in the past.

Consequences of Altering Past Events

Important events played out in one universe in a nuanced dance of cause and effect, with slight variations. Alex saw variations on well-known faces and locations, each one serving as a reminder of the countless paths that could be taken from even the slightest temporal prods. A kaleidoscope of worlds affected by past decisions was created by the ripple effects of even the smallest changes throughout the multiverse.

Repercussions of Changing Historical Events

The temptation to change history became too strong, and Alex quickly realized the serious ramifications of doing so. Once only a theoretical idea, the butterfly effect came to be and its wings caused ripples that went well beyond the point of change.

Trying to make amends for a personal tragedy had unanticipated consequences because fate has surprising ways of weaving itself together. The small changes in the past caused foes to become allies and friends to become strangers. Rewriting history had unintended repercussions that tore through the veneer of familiarity and created a new reality marked by the scars of temporal intervention.

Over time, the burden of responsibility increased with every journey. The protagonist struggled with moral conundrums brought on by the ability to alter entire universes in addition to personal struggles. Was it fair for one person to control the course of innumerable lives like a puppeteer?
With the unfolding of parallel worlds resembling pages in a cosmic book, Alex took comfort in the knowledge that everything is interrelated. The enigma of the time traveler grew beyond the confines of several timelines, creating a story that beyond comprehension. Parallel universe research was just getting started, but it held great promise for discoveries that would call into question the fundamental structure of reality.

Chapter 4: Historical Threads

Alex was driven by his unwavering quest for historical mystery through a maze of eras where mysteries awaited discovery.

The protagonist sets out to conduct research in several historical eras.

Alex felt drawn to far-off places and eras gone by the resonant whispers of old mysteries. The protagonist searched for hints to an occult relic that contained the echoes of a vanished civilization amid the crowded marketplaces of ancient Babylon. As Alex made his way through the intricate labyrinth of a city lost to the passage of time, the air was heavy with the aroma of exotic spices.

Bagpipes played in the background as the protagonist searched for a buried scroll, its contents shrouded in the shadow of Highland legends, amidst the undulating hills of ancient Scotland. Alex made his way through the shadows generated by lochs and castles, piecing together the clues left by a mysterious society that existed for generations.

Discover a Centuries-Old Conspiracy

A massive plot spanning millennia started to come into view as all the historical puzzle pieces came together. A complex web of deception, skillfully interwoven across history, united seemingly unrelated incidents into a captivating whole. The hidden society—once believed to be limited to particular historical periods—has shown itself to be the mastermind behind history.

Through deciphering secret codes hidden in Renaissance illuminated manuscripts, the main character tracked the impact of this covert organization. The conspiracy left its stamp on important turning points in human history, from the sumptuous courts of Versailles to the smoke-filled salons of Enlightenment philosophers. Alex felt the strings of history's big stage being pulled by a dark entity.

With every new discovery, the stakes become higher since the conspiracy's entanglements went beyond time and into the core of the protagonist's being. Allies had ulterior motives, and friends unintentionally turned into pawns. The past, which had previously offered comfort, was now burdened by a plot to alter fate itself.

Alex was at the brink of danger and disclosure in the maze of historical intrigue. The genuine essence of the plot grew large, casting doubt on the time-traveling mystery's very roots. The past grew darker as the protagonist continued on, and the echoes of an enduring conspiracy murmured truths that would define the chapters to come.

Chapter 5: Dangers of the Past

As the adversary's cunning scheme came to pass, the dark undercurrent of temporal manipulation became more prominent and cast a shadow across time.

Expose the Antagonist's Dark Scheme Including Time Dilation

An evil power surfaced from the shadowy corners of the temporal tapestry. The enemy, hidden behind a curtain of secrecy, hatched a scheme that went beyond reason and decency. Alex discovered the dark reality as he dug further into the mysteries: the enemy intended to use time itself for their own evil ends.

Words of a time machine, a relic of mysterious strength, reverberated through the halls of time. By manipulating time itself, the enemy hoped to use this relic as a weapon and change reality to suit their sinister plans. Such manipulation had disastrous results that threatened to tear apart the very fabric of existence.

Increase Tension as Their Intent Becomes More Discernible
As the antagonist's intentions became more apparent, the tension increased. The temporal threats carried a burden greater than self-interest; they aspired to alter the fundamental laws that guided the cosmos. Alex battled with the understanding that the fight against this temporal evil was a defense of reality itself, as much as a fight for his own existence.

The stakes grew increasingly intense as the antagonist's plans came to light. The mysterious individual threw aside the fine balance that kept the past, present, and future in balance in an attempt to impose their own sense of order on the chaos of time. A disastrous domino effect was created by the consequences of failure, which threatened to spread beyond the protagonist's own timeline and into other realities.

It was a literal and metaphorical race against time for the protagonist to foil the antagonist's evil schemes. The mysteries of time got ever more enigmatic with each new insight, and each stride forward was a risky dance with the brink of oblivion.
The conflict between the protagonist and adversary would intensify in the following chapters, and the extent of the temporal dangers would become clear, casting doubt on the core of the time-traveling enigma that united them.

Chapter 6 :The Battle Against Illusions

As time sped by them, Alex felt the weight of duty rise. Finding a way to prevent temporal paradoxes became their top concern because the timeline's precarious equilibrium depended on it.

Their makeshift laboratory was covered in charts and graphs that illustrated the intricate dance of cause and effect. Dr. Marlow, the team's resident temporal physicist, frowned and stated, "Every action in the past has ripple effects, and if we're not cautious, we risk creating paradoxes that could shatter the very fabric of time."

The team reviewed historical data and laboriously tweaked their time-travel devices as they raced against the clock. Every decision had the potential to be contradicted, like stray threads threatening to unravel the tapestry of existence itself.

But when they delved more into the temporal intricacies, they were unable to escape the inevitable collisions between the past and the future. Dealing with the fallout became a harrowing journey through moments when recollections of their own interventions echoed.

They had witnessed the unanticipated outcomes of a minor alteration made to a historical event. They had no idea how the effects would ripple out over time, shifting allies and altering the international landscape. Their attempts to force

reforms were met with resistance from the past, which took
revenge for their meddling.

They raced across ages, and different futures appeared in front of them. Some showed them utopias that offered the hope of a better society, while others showed depressing scenes brought about by even the slightest disturbances. The consequences of their actions reverberated through every instant as the past and future collided to create a symphony of temporal echoes.

In an effort to make things right before the discrepancies got worse, the group was compelled to investigate the aberrations. The urgency of their mission grew as they came upon temporal storms, which were spinning vortexes that threatened to engulf them in a maelstrom of conflicting timelines.

The basic truth that meddling with time has consequences with every step they take was difficult for them to accept. Their choices had long-lasting effects, and the past was resistant to change. The group raced against paradoxes, teetering on the edge of time, knowing that safeguarding the present would equally mean endangering the stability of the past and the promise of the future.

Chapter 7: Betrayals and Allies

Alex and the group came up unexpected allies from several timelines as they negotiated the complex web of time. Every ally contributed a different viewpoint and set of abilities, a collision between the past and the future in the present.

One such ally came from the eighteenth century, a bright inventor who had used simple but clever gadgets to unravel the secrets of time travel. With the knowledge of ages in his eyes, he developed into a useful asset who could connect the gaps in technology between different eras.

Another ally, a cybernetically augmented agent knowledgeable in sophisticated temporal theories, appeared from the far future. Their encounters with this mysterious entity made it difficult to distinguish between humans and machines and gave them a peek of what lay ahead for humanity's evolution.

But amid the friendships that were formed during time, trust problems grew like a silent plague. Time travel by its very nature breeds cynicism, and the team began to wonder about the intentions of their newfound friends. There was an air of trepidation in their secret gatherings, with rumors of possible betrayals ringing true.

Personal motivations entwined with the overarching objective of maintaining the timeline as the team dug deeper into their task. As a result of competing interests, loyalty in this age-old dance grew brittle. The allies balanced cooperation with self-preservation, each with an agenda defined by the eras from which they originated.

In the shadowy corners of past landscapes, clandestine discussions took place where alliances were tested and new ones were established. The team's once unwavering trust was suddenly tenuous, and each choice they made became a calculated play in the temporal chess match they were caught up in.

Every step they took was tinged with tension as the echoes of possible betrayals echoed through the passages of time. The crew had to contend with internal conflict resulting from misgivings and suspicions in addition to external threats as they raced against contradictions.

Alex and the group came to the realization that solving the mysteries of time would entail not only understanding the complexities of temporal physics but also negotiating the treacherous terrain of human nature over ages in this constantly changing environment of allies and betrayals. Not only did the past and future meet in events, but their minds and emotions also did.

Section 8: The Last Face-to-Face

After their chronological journey came to an end, Alex and the group were ready for the big reveal—the last showdown. The consequences of what they did resonated as they moved through the passage of time, preparing the stage for an intergenerational feud.

After they'd set off the disturbances, temporal storms raged, swirling shapes. There was a visible indication of the impending catastrophe in the form of a warping and twisting of reality itself. A sense of urgency and the weight of duty that hung over them like a timeless shadow kept the team moving forward.

Their enemies were not only outside dangers but also the same paradoxes they were trying to solve. Views of parallel timelines played out like spectral apparitions as they got closer to the temporal disturbance's epicenter. This pivotal moment brought together the outcomes of their interventions, the alliances formed, and the trust that was put to the test.

The team faced mirror images of themselves in this last encounter—different versions molded by different decisions and unanticipated outcomes. A strange meeting with the plethora of possibilities that arose from their journey through time caused the air to crackle with tension as they faced reflections of their own ambitions and concerns.

The person who orchestrated the pandemonium turned out to be the temporal architect, a mysterious individual who was tinkering with the threads of time. Their true intentions were revealed when the crew faced this mysterious enemy, however their motivations remained a mystery.

The conflict went beyond the material and into the domains of morality and philosophy. The group debated if making sacrifices that went beyond moral lines was necessary to maintain the timeline as they considered the ramifications of their choices. The boundaries of good and wrong became hazy during the last confrontation, leaving them to negotiate the murky waters of temporal morality.

The forming and breaking of alliances was vital in the whirling storm of temporal energies. Now, the trust they had developed throughout their voyage was put to the ultimate test. The group faced internal conflicts stemming from ambiguity and doubt in addition to external opponents, raising the possibility of betrayals.

The whole fabric of time seemed to hold its breath as the final encounter reached its peak. The decisions they took at this critical juncture would ripple down the halls of history and into the uncertain future they aimed to mold, ultimately determining the outcome of their quest to solve the riddles of time.

Chapter 9: The Culmination

The squad experienced a quiet calm as the momentary storm passed. With great care and elegance, the temporal dilemma was resolved, with every adjustment becoming a stitch in the history of time. Once caught in a state of chaotic discord, the past and future have now established a peaceful equilibrium.

The group's coordinated efforts, led by friends from many times, created a peaceful stillness. Once chaotic and erratic, the temporal currents now flowed with a fresh order. There was a communal sigh of relief as the crisis that had threatened to throw reality into turmoil was avoided.

Relief and a sense of success accompanied the resolution, but the revelation that was just around the corner suggested that they still had more work to do before fully comprehending the mysteries they had solved. The time-traveling mystery's ultimate explanation emerged like a tapestry made of fate's strands.

After a moment of collective insight, the group realized that they were the ones who had created the temporal disruptions. The very crisis the team was trying to avert had been unintentionally brought on by the future selves' desperate attempts to control a particular course of events.

The insight provided a clearer understanding of the complexities of causality. The group struggled with the weight of their decisions, which had an impact on them personally as well as throughout time. The puzzles they set out to answer were mirror images of their own deeds; the voyage through time had been an exercise in self-imposed punishment, an attempt to comprehend the fallout from controlling fate.

There were unanswered questions as the crew processed the information. What kind of future were they hoping to escape, and what kind of costs were they willing to pay to keep it safe? They were forced to consider the moral ramifications of their task as the lines between saviors and manipulators became more hazy.

In a time of deep reflection, the resolve and revelation came together. Once motivated by the need to save the deadline, the team found itself at a standstill between accountability and responsibility. The riddles of time were transformed from mysterious phantoms to the reflections of decisions made and the reverberations of repercussions acknowledged.

Following the temporal crisis, as the group reflected on the actual purpose of their expedition, they realized that the final discovery had nothing to do with comprehending time, but rather with accepting the intricacy of their own existence within the enormous range of temporal possibilities.

Chapter 10: Wrap-Up

The team found themselves in the aftermath, evaluating the terrain of time they had traversed, as the echoes of the temporal crisis subsided. The resolution restored some measure of order, but the traces of their trip continued to exist like ghosts of the past.

Their interventions left tiny impressions on the world around them, reverberating from changes made and paradoxes avoided. Timelines had shifted, history had been pushed aside, and the past and future had found a precarious balance. The squad was on the cusp of a new era, its resolve now hardened by the test of time.

Once united by the urgency of their task, the partners from many timelines now had to deal with the unknown. They were kept together by the trust they developed in the furnace of difficulties, but the realization of their own future selves left them feeling reflective for a long time. The group had taken on the role of architects of their own fate, and there was an obvious burden of duty hanging over them.

After their time-traveling adventure came to an end, the group considered the lessons they had learned, including the need to strike a careful balance between intervention and preservation, the repercussions of exercising temporal power, and the moral issues raised by time travel.

A feeling of resolution descended upon the group as they broke up and went back to their own times. Once veiled in mystery, the mysteries of time now stood exposed as reflections of their own decisions. The temporal crisis was resolved, and it was a win not only over external dangers but also over internal tensions and doubts.

But in the midst of the resolution, there was a faint glimmer of promise. The now-stabilized fabric of time held hints of yet-to-be-discovered strands and unknown regions. Even though they were geographically apart, the group had an implicit awareness that the voyage through time was far from finished.

The epilogue teased to unanswered questions and uncharted territory in the temporal landscape, leaving room for possible spin-offs or sequels. The mysterious allies, the consequences of their actions, and the ever-present draw of the unknown future drew readers in and encouraged them to envision the untold tales that lay ahead after the last few pages.

A sense of both closure and suspense persisted as the final words of the time-traveling mystery reverberated throughout the story, demonstrating the intricacy of time and the limitless opportunities that awaited anyone brave enough to venture into its mysterious domains.